The Magic School Bus®

SEES STARS

A BOOK ABOUT STARS

SCHOLASTIC INC.

New York   Toronto   London   Auckland   Sydney
Mexico City   New Delhi   Hong Kong   Buenos Aires

From an episode of the animated TV series
produced by Scholastic Entertainment Inc.
Based on *The Magic School Bus* books
written by Joanna Cole and illustrated by Bruce Degen.

TV tie-in book adaptation by Nancy White and illustrated by Art Ruiz.
TV script written by Noel MacNeal.

ISBN 0-590-18732-5

24 23 22 21 20 19 18   6 7 8 9/0

Printed in the U.S.A.

If you ever get Ms. Frizzle for a teacher, take this warning from me. Get ready for something wild and crazy to happen any time you hear these three little words:

"To the bus!"

For example, take the time Dorothy Ann was sick and had to stay home on her birthday. Tim was working on the birthday present we were going to give her — a model of the sun that played "You Are My Sunshine" when you wound it up.

Just when Tim was putting the final touches on D.A.'s present, the phone rang. It was D.A.! She wanted us to come over to see her new telescope. We said we'd be over as soon as Ms. Frizzle came back from her teachers meeting. Then . . . enter the Friz!

Ah . . . Good afternoon, class!

"Take a look, Ms. Frizzle," said Tim, who couldn't wait to show off our musical model of the sun. But then something terrible happened. The model fell and smashed on the floor.

"It's too late to make another present," said Phoebe. "What are we going to do?"

As if answering Phoebe's question, the TV clicked on. It was on one of those channels where you can buy things, and this weird guy named Horace Cope was saying you could actually buy a star — for just seven dollars! He said only three stars were left.

We were all taking out our dollar bills when Keesha shouted, "Wait a minute! I'm not spending my money on anything I haven't checked out myself!"

"Keesha's right," the Friz agreed. "We don't have to buy a star sight unseen." And then she said those three words.

To the bus!

I think we're going star shopping.

Couldn't we just go to the mall?

In my old school, we got pencils for our birthdays.

We all got on the Magic School Bus — or should I say the Magic Space Bus?

To reach the stars, you have to get way past Mars!

When we looked down, we couldn't believe our eyes. We could see the whole earth. It looked huge at first, but then it looked smaller and smaller as we got farther away. The same with the moon. Then we couldn't see the earth or the moon at all, and the sun was so far away it looked like — well . . . it looked just like a tiny star.

Then Ms. Frizzle told us something amazing — our sun really is a star! It looks bigger than the other stars because it's so much closer to Earth.

Soon, we were cruising through space. The view was fantastic!

"Gee, look at all those teeny-weeny stars," said Phoebe. "I wonder if they'll get bigger when we get closer — like the earth and the moon did."

"They'd better," said Keesha. "We need some way to tell them apart."

We turned on the space bus TV, and guess who was on? That good old stellar seller, Horace Cope!

"Now, you're probably asking how you can pick out a star because they all look alike, right?" said Horace. "Wrong! There are lots of different kinds of stars."

"For instance," he continued, "take this little baby. Only two million years old! Believe it or not, that's really young for a star!"

"To see it yourself," said Horace, "you'd have to fly at a speed of five hundred million miles an hour, and it would still take you about eighty years to get there."

Ms. Frizzle hit the controls, and we zoomed out into space. Maybe it would take Horace Cope eighty years to reach the baby star, but then he doesn't have the Friz for a teacher — and he doesn't have a Magic Space Bus.

As we approached a beautiful swirling cloud, Ms. Frizzle said, "Hmmm . . . That baby star should be around here somewhere, but it's hard to tell with all this dust and gas."

"Dust and gas?" said Keesha. "Is that what these weird clouds are made of?"

Phoebe looked worried. "This is not a good place for a baby," she said.

But Ms. Frizzle told us, "On the contrary, kids, it's the best place for a baby!"

A baby star, that is!

"Hey," shouted Wanda, "there's the baby star!"

"For a baby, it sure is humongous!" said Arnold.

"It's actually on the small side," Ms. Frizzle told us. "Only about half the size of our sun."

Tim was ready to buy. "Let's call up Horace Cope and get it for D.A."

But Keesha still wasn't sure.

Phoebe agreed with Keesha. "Poor thing," she said. "It looks like it's got gas."

"Very good, Phoebe! All stars have gas," explained Ms. Frizzle. "That's what they're made of! But this baby just hasn't settled down yet. It's still kind of wild."

Now Keesha was sure. "No way!" she said. "I'm not spending a dime on this star. It's too young and too wild. I want something bigger and brighter, with no dust around it. A star we can trust — like our own sun."

I want a star that has a planet or two!

Back on the old TV, Horace Cope seemed to hear every word we were saying. "No problem!" he said. "Remember, there are still two stars left! And one of them is a five-billion-year-old middle-ager, right in the prime of its life. Planets at no extra charge!"

The middle-aged star sounded perfect! But the space bus computer told us it was one hundred million million miles away. (In case you were wondering, that's 100,000,000,000,000!)

No problem for the Friz! "Seats, everyone, and buckle up," she said. Then she got that look in her eye as she launched us into hyperdrive.

We have to travel far
to get to this star!

When the space bus slowed down, we could see our star.

"There it is, Keesha!" said Tim. "Just the kind of star we want."

Keesha still wasn't convinced. "It looks OK," she said, "but I want to be sure it's different from the baby star."

Of course, the Friz thought that was a great idea.

Let's take a closer look.

To get a closer look at our star, we got into the special star shuttle. Lucky for us, the shuttle came equipped with sunglasses — or should I say starglasses?

We all waited to hear what Keesha would say. Finally, she spoke.

"I like the color a lot better," she said. "And it seems a lot calmer. No dust clouds around it, either. And I can see at least two planets. Wow, this star looks just like our sun!"

Let's buy it!

Everyone was really excited . . . until we got back
to the space bus and heard Horace's voice on the TV.

SOLD!

"But I haven't even called in yet," said Keesha.
"I guess someone bought it first," said Arnold.
We all felt pretty bad until Carlos reminded us,
"There's still one star left."

Don't give up yet, guys!

All eyes — and ears — were glued to the TV. This was our last chance to get D.A. a star for her birthday.

"That's right, folks," Horace was saying. "Just one star left, and I've saved the best for last — a genuine red supergiant! Twenty million years old and a hundred times bigger than the sun! What's more, I'll take fifty cents off the price if somebody buys it in the next minute. Check it out!"

As you can guess, with the Friz at the controls, we reached the red supergiant in a wink, just like magic. (Our bus isn't called Magic for nothing!) Keesha looked out the window. "Well, it's certainly the biggest star we've seen. And I like the color," she said. "It doesn't have any planets, but there are no dust clouds, either. And it's no wild baby."

Tim called in and ordered the red supergiant. "We did it!" he said. "We got D.A. a star that's bigger and brighter than all the others!"

Ralphie looked worried. "Hey, wait a minute!" he said. "If it's so much bigger, how come we got it so cheap?"

"Yeah," said Wanda. "Horace Cope did seem in a hurry to sell the red supergiant."

"Do you think something's wrong with it?" asked Keesha. "I don't see anything wrong."

"As my old friend Li Brarian always says," said Ms. Frizzle, "you can't tell a book by its cover. Let's take a peek inside with the sneakapeekatron."

On the sneakapeekatron screen, we could actually see right inside our star. This is what we saw:

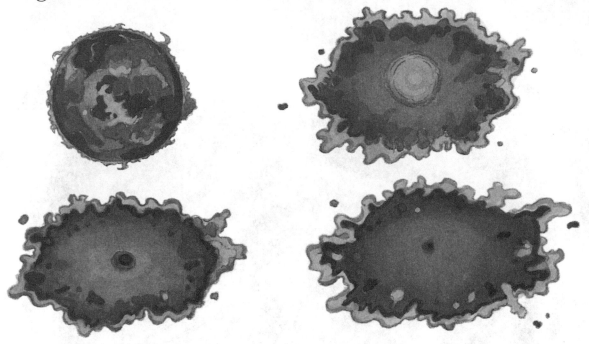

"Is it just me," said Ralphie, "or are the insides of our star shrinking?"

"Who cares what's going on inside," said Tim,
"as long as it looks OK on the outside?"
But just then . . .

After all our hard work, D.A.'s big,
beautiful star exploded into smithereens!

"Why did our star explode?" asked Keesha. "It looked okay on the outside. It was bigger and brighter . . ."

"Well," interrupted Phoebe, "it was twenty million years old."

"A stellar observation, Phoebe," said Ms. Frizzle. "Stars do grow old and go out. Some go out with a bang. They're called supernovas."

"Super mess," said Carlos. "All that's left of D.A.'s star is a big cloud of dust and gas."

"Hey, wait," said Keesha. "This looks a lot like the place where we found the baby star. I'll bet another baby star is about to be born right here!"

"That's right!" said Phoebe. "Stars are made out of hot gasses squeezed together in a ball!"

Then we figured out the whole idea.

Gasses are squeezed hot enough . . .

. . . to make a new baby star shine.

"Very interesting, but we still need a present for D.A.," Wanda reminded us. "It's too bad we can't gather up all this gas and dust and squeeze it together to make D.A. a new star."

"Who says we can't, Wanda!" said Ms. Frizzle. "Normally, it would take about a million years to make a star — but since we have a magic bus, we can make it happen now!"

Thanks to the Magic Space Bus — PRESTO! A brand-new star named Dorothy Ann was shining in the sky. Mission accomplished!

When we arrived at Dorothy Ann's house, D.A. was looking through the new telescope she got for her birthday.

"You're just in time to see a brand-new star in the sky!" she said.

"Actually, D.A.," said Keesha, "that's your birthday present. We named it Dorothy Ann in your honor."

"But how? I don't understand." For once, D.A. was confused.

"That's a long story," said Ms. Frizzle. "A story filled with dust and gas, with heat and . . ."

"Happy birthday, D.A.," we all shouted together.

Letters from Our Readers

Dear Editor,
Who are you kidding? No one can visit the stars. But if we could, how long would it take?
Your pal,
Lon Journey

Dear Lon,
You're right! The stars are too far away to reach with today's spacecraft. If we could travel that far, it would take a whole lifetime to get there and back. Unless you traveled faster than the speed of light — and that's impossible.
The Editor

Dear Editor,
I'm concerned. You know how you said our sun was a star? And stars go out? Will our sun go out, too?
Signed,
Scared of the Dark

Dear Scared,
Yes, our sun will go out — but not for a very long time. It's been shining for more than four billion years — and it has another four or five billion to go. So lighten up!
The Editor

Pictures in the Sky:
An Activity for Parents and Kids

Since ancient times, people have seen pictures in different groups of stars. These groups of stars are called constellations.

You've probably heard of a group of stars called the Big Dipper. It would look like a long-handled cup if you drew lines between the stars — like a giant connect-the-dots picture. The two stars in the front of the cup point to the North Star in the handle of the Little Dipper. The dippers are parts of the constellations Ursa Major (Big Bear) and Ursa Minor (Little Bear). In Greek mythology, Ursa Major was once a beautiful nymph, Callisto, and Ursa Minor was her son, Arcas. Zeus, king of the gods, loved Callisto, and when his angry wife tried to kill her, he turned Callisto into a bear. Not knowing the bear was his mother, Arcas tried to kill her. So Zeus turned Arcas into a bear and put them both in the sky.

The ancient Greeks thought another constellation looked like a beautiful princess in a story. Princess Andromeda's mother bragged that her daughter was more beautiful than the daughters of the god of the sea. The god was so angry that he sent a giant sea monster to devour everyone in the kingdom. The monster was about to eat poor Andromeda when the hero Perseus flew by on his winged horse, killed the monster, and rescued the princess.

See if you can find these groups of stars. Find other constellations, too — and read their stories.